Journey Through the Old Testament

Grounded and Growing Through His Word

By Dale Hansen

Celine

Thanks for your support!

Dale

This book is dedicated to my wife Patti, for her inspiration, encouragement and her ongoing support. She put in many hours of editing and rereading.

To my readers for their support.

To my covers illustrator: Mark.

To my editors:

Patti

Jaye

Dave

Terry

Joe

Introduction

Often, we are too busy to spend time in God's Word or to spend any time in prayer with Him. God wants a simple relationship with Him for "apart from me you can do nothing." John 15:5, NIV. It is not about us but about God and putting Him first in all areas of our lives.

Sometimes our Bible devotions give us too much information for one day or we forget what we learned the rest of the day. My books allow us to spend one week with the same set of verses which you can pray and think about during the week. Every day would be great but with our busyness, three to five days would be good for a start. Our goal is daily time with Him, and I believe 10 minutes a day is better than two hours one day a week! This moves you toward really knowing, understanding and living the verses, along with a key verse, a doable application and a personal thought. Three key areas are:

1) Time reading and studying HIs Word.

2)Time to pray and using a prayer list.

3) Have a list of key verses for reference and prayer.

This can be used by yourself, with a partner or in an accountability or study group.

This book focuses on the Old Testament and covers all the books and many experiences of the people in the Bible. Many verses are part of an Old Testament overview I put together over 25 years ago. I used it for myself to better understand the timing, flow and God's purpose of the Old Testament. I also used this for small group Bible studies. This version is revised with additional verses and written as weekly devotions from Genesis to Malachi. This book also includes some additional verse references including dates for key events when the Israelites were led by their first three kings (Saul, David and Solomon), when they became a divided kingdom, disappearing into exile and having God restore them by the end of the Old Testament. God restored them back to Jerusalem through rebuilding the city wall and rebuilding their relationship with Him. Malachi finishes the Old Testament and anticipates God's messenger preparing for the coming of the Savior.

Read it! Learn It! Share it!

Dale Hansen

www,groundedandgrowingweekly.com

WEEK 1   Genesis 1:1-2:4   Focus: 2:3

Overview: Genesis tells of God creating this world. He created the lights, the waters, the land, the plants, the trees, the animals and the stars. This took Him six days, and He rested on the seventh day.

Focus: God made everything in nature for us and Himself to enjoy. We see many varieties of plants, flowers, birds and animals. He then rested from His creation on the seventh day (2:3). He decided this day would be holy and set apart and this day would have its own commandment: "Remember to observe the Sabbath day by keeping it holy" (Exodus 20:8).

How to Apply: Have you ever scheduled some rest time into your schedule? Have you ever put a big R on a day on your calendar? During this week, do one or more from this list:

- walk in the park.
- read a book.
- go to a movie with a friend.
- take a nap.
- start a book of the Bible.

One of my favorites things to do is when I am out at night and I look up for the moon. I am always thanking our great God for the beauty of the moon when the sky is clear and the moon is full. A less than full moon will reveal the stars in the night sky as a reminder of how awesome God is. The moon is still there when it is cloudy. God is still with us on cloudy and difficult days.

WEEK 2   Genesis 2:5-25   Focus: 2:18

Overview: God then made man from the dust of the ground, and the man became a living person. This was all good and man was to care for the earth. God was very pleased with man but He saw that man was alone and needed a companion. God saw the need for companionship and relationships.

Focus: God realized we would need help, support and encouragement along the way. God created the woman from the man's rib. This is why the man leaves his mother and father and joins his wife. The two are united as one.

How to Apply: The relationship of the first man and woman impacts our lives to this day. Relationships are important to us and we need to work on them to help sustain them. There are three or four guys that I have known for years, and I try to stay in touch with them even if only a few calls and e-mails each year. When we do talk, we ask how our spiritual lives are going. During this week, review your current relationships with God (Psalm 42:1), family and friends as below:

1) First, ensure your relationship with God is solid and continues to grow.
2) Second, ensure you are right with your spouse.
3) Third, ask God to reveal a special friend relationship which needs attention.

Overview: Today we continue to blame others for our wrong actions and the resulting consequences. It is hard to admit we are wrong. Even if men are lost, we are not lost and we certainly will not ask for directions. (Sorry guys.) The serpent (the devil) told Eve she could eat the fruit off the tree of life, and Eve told Adam he could eat the fruit. They both sinned against God.

Focus: Adam blamed Eve for his wrong choice (3:12), and Eve blamed the serpent (3:13) for their disobedience. We make many choices every day. Some are routine while others are between right and wrong. We need to ensure we are walking with God daily in order to make the right choices and to know what He wants us to do.

How to Apply: Time in God's Word gives us the knowledge and strength to obey Him. When my wife and I faced infertility, we sought His guidance and His peace rather than placing blame on Him for something we did not understand. Later, God blessed us with two awesome adopted daughters. During this coming week, start by asking God for help with your daily choices. Read and pray through Psalm 51:10-12. Ask Him for forgiveness for a wrong choice and for a willingness to obey Him every day. Think of a choice or decision you need to make soon and ask God for direction. Consider every area of your life.

WEEK 4   Genesis 6:1-22   Focus: 6:9

Overview: The earth continued to populate and grow with humans. God saw their wicked thoughts and actions. There was violence and depravity everywhere and God was so sad He made humans. This was not what He wanted when He first created Adam and Eve. He wanted to destroy the whole earth, but there was one righteous man during this time. His name was Noah and he was true to God and blameless before God.

Focus: Genesis tells us Noah followed God's will, was obedient and had a close relationship with God (6:9). Noah was obedient despite all the sinful actions and sinful people around him. God said He would destroy all on earth except Noah and his family. God gave directions to build an ark for his family and two pairs of each animal.

How to apply: Sometimes I whine when God wants me to do something I am not sure I want or can do. I think of Noah's obedience to build an ark and ponder on what he thought of this monumental task. How did Noah stay focused with the negative influences around him? Some scholars say it took up to 100 years for Noah to build the ark. In Romans 12:2, Paul tells us not to "copy the behavior and customs of this world". He challenges us to change the way we think and allow God to transform us. During this week, meditate on Genesis 6:9 and Romans 12:2. Think and pray about how God is transforming you and keeping you focused. Compile a list of Bible reference verses for prayer and future encouragement.

WEEK 5   Genesis 12:1-20   Focus: 12:1

Overview: This chapter begins the story of Abram (later called Abraham). God called him to leave his family, relatives, friends and his homeland without revealing his final destination. God promised Abram blessings for his family, the nation of Israel and for future generations if he would obey and trust in God.

Focus: He left his homeland with no specific details on his trip. Abram had to be afraid, but his faith was strong and he trusted in God. He responded with immediate obedience and asked no questions. His trust in God's direction was complete. How would you have responded? I would have at least asked a few questions regarding the details.

How to Apply: We have moved twice through company transfers and did a lot of planning and received some details. We prayed through both moves and both went well despite the first move being away from family, relatives, friends and our home state. Have you ever been instructed to a task or direction by God? Always seek God's direction through prayer before you commit. During this week, think about past and future decisions and pray about what God may ask you to do. Confirm through prayer that you are following God's will and let go to let Him lead. Reread verses 12:1, 4 and 7.

WEEK 6   Genesis 22:1-24   Focus: 22:15-18

Overview: Abraham's faith and trust in God were very strong. In the previous devotion, God said He would bless Abraham and make him a leader of a great nation. God now tests Abraham's faithfulness and obedience. God tells Abraham to sacrifice Isaac, his only son.

Focus: Abraham got up the next morning and made immediate preparations for his journey with his son and servants. Abraham wholeheartedly obeyed God. He tied Isaac to the altar and just as he was ready to kill his son, the Lord stopped him.

How to Apply: God intervenes, provides a sacrifice and sees Abraham's obedience regardless of the consequences (22:10-12). How far are we willing to act to obey God? How often do we question God when He tells us to do something? My wife and I obeyed Him when we chose our church after our first move. After attending a few, we narrowed the choice down to two churches. One was like our previous church but through prayer, we stepped from our comfort zone and chose the other church which was very different. We were blessed for the four years we were there. During this week, spend time praying through verses 15 to 18. Evaluate areas of your life where you need to obey him. Pick two to pray through and work on.

Overview: Joseph's story begins in Genesis 37. His story is about waiting on God's timing and knowing God did not leave him. His life began teaching us how not to build relationships. He first would tell his father, Jacob, the bad things his brothers were doing (37:2). Jacob gave Joseph a beautiful robe and was very partial to Joseph (37:3) which his brothers noted. Joseph had dreams where his brothers bowed down to him (37:5-8).

Focus: After telling his brothers of the dreams, they would not say a kind word to him and they sought vengeance. They discussed how to kill him. Through a series of events, Joseph is sold into slavery, spends some years in jail and comes to the house of the officer of Pharaoh, king of Egypt. From the time Joseph was sold in slavery God had His plan viewing the larger picture. Joseph showed patience as he waited on God to work for 22 years.

How to Apply: My wife and I struggled with infertility despite the fact that we wanted children. The ongoing process took over two years. We felt frustrated but trusted. Through prayers and tests and phone calls, God blessed us beyond our wildest dreams (Ephesians 3:20). We adopted two daughters three years apart and my wife did not gain a pound during both adoptions. During this week, pray and ask God reveal himself to you in an area you have been waiting and praying about. Use verse Ephesians 3:20, showing you that God can work beyond our highest expectations and dreams.

WEEK 8   Genesis 45:1 - 46:4   Focus: 45:5-7

Overview: God worked through Joseph beyond what Joseph could have imagined (Ephesians 3:20). After 22 years, Joseph became the second most important person in Egypt. His brothers were shocked when Joseph revealed himself to them. They had come to Egypt due to the famine in the lands (45:1-4). God used Joseph to prepare Egypt for the famine that God had revealed to him. The Pharaoh heard about the reunion with his brothers and requested that Joseph's father, Jacob, and the rest of his family come to Egypt.

Focus: Jacob came to Egypt from Canaan with his 11 other sons. Jacob was the son of Abraham. God gave Jacob a vision through a dream. God told Jacob that he would become a great nation while in Egypt and would someday return to the land of Canaan (46:1-4). In Hebrew, Jacob is called Israel.

How to Apply: In the midst of Joseph's trials, God had allowed all the events to work for His good (Romans 8:28). Through a unique set of circumstances, God reunited Joseph with his father and brothers to help them survive the famine. This sets up Israel living in Egypt for Moses to come and help return them to Canaan. Just as our infertility and adoptions over 3 years, God was orchestrating behind the scenes to connect the dots. He sees the bigger picture while we try to manage today. During this week, mark Romans 8:28, and pray through this verse in one or two struggles you may be going through. Pray that you will continue to love God and seek His purpose for your life.

WEEK 9   Exodus 2:1 – 3:10   Focus: 2:10

Overview: Chapter 2 of Exodus starts the story of Moses, the Hebrew. He was raised in the house of the Pharaoh of Egypt. He would become one of the great men and leaders from the Bible. Moses murdered an Egyptian who was beating on a Hebrew and the Hebrews wanted nothing to do with him since he was raised as an Egyptian. Moses fled into the wilderness and away from the Egyptians who wanted him for the murder.

Focus: Forty years later, God called him from a "burning bush" (3:3). The Hebrews had become slaves under this current Pharaoh. God heard the cries of His people enduring slavery and hardships. God called Moses to lead His people out of Egypt and to the Promised Land (Canaan). God believed Moses was ready for this task. From the start, Moses questioned God if he was ready and tried to say no or get help seven times.

How to Apply: Have you ever been called by God and hesitated at the beginning? Our first move was scary. When we first relocated off the east coast, we sometimes went back and forth about whether this was God at work. We were moving from family, friends and our church family, but we trusted God and the move turned out to be better than we could have imagined. God was with us starting up in a new location. God did tell Moses who He was and that He would be with him all the time. During this week, read 3:12 and trust God in a choice or decision you may be considering and ask for His direction.

Overview: Moses did lead the people out of Egypt. In the wilderness, they came to Mt. Sinai. God gave them laws and instructions for living. Many additional instructions are found in the book of Leviticus (7:37-38). God also had more instructions and a census of the people in the book of Numbers (1:46). At Mt. Sinai, God gave the Ten Commandments to Moses.

Focus: The first four commandments involve our relationship to God. He must be the top priority in our daily lives. Nothing can take His place in our hearts. The last six reveal how we are to relate to our family, friends and neighbors. Specifically, number four reminds us on how to treat the Sabbath day and number ten tells us not to covet anything of our neighbors.

How to Apply: In our own lives, we must make sure there is nothing in the way with our relationship to God (1 John 5:21). Some things can be beneficial, but they must not monopolize our time or be our top priority. These can include hobbies, TV, music, Facebook, texting, cars and relationships. About 10 years ago, I decided to only watch college football and was tired of watching the NFL for a few reasons. I picked up some available time on Sundays, Mondays and Thursdays! During this coming week, pray through 1 John 5:21 and Exodus 20:8 and ask God to reveal an area of your life that needs to be reduced, tweaked or eliminated.

WEEK 11   Leviticus 7:1-38   Focus: 7:37-38

Overview: The book of Leviticus is a tedious read about all the instructions God gave to Moses regarding the handling of offerings to the Lord: offerings for sin, peace, grain, burnt, guilt and ordination. All offerings presented to God must come from the herds and flocks of the people (1:1-2). These instructions needed to be followed obediently by the Jews.

Focus: Have you ever needed to follow instructions? Have you ever not followed instructions? Instructions that I have followed range from putting a toy together to putting a grill together to putting a faucet on a sink. My favorites include requiring a screw driver to assemble and by the end, all of my tools are used. One time I did put a grill together and had three or four screws still left. Currently, the grill still works! Sometimes we just say we can do this without instructions. Just like sometimes we do not like to read the directions because we "know" where we are going.

How to apply: God's Word is our instruction manual for following God and how to live our lives for Him. God wants us to give our hearts to Him, to live for Him and to be equipped in serving Him. The Bible (Basic Instructions Before Leaving Earth) teaches right from wrong and for us to meditate on the instructions. Today our offerings to God include our hearts, our lives and our service to Him. During this week, reread 7:37-38 and meditate on 2 Timothy 3:16-17.

WEEK 12   Numbers 14:1-45   Focus: 14:8-9

Overview: The book of Numbers continues with instructions from Moses to the people. These include a census, tribe organization, the unique Levites/ priests responsibilities and additional offerings. In the middle of this book, the Jews have reached the promised land after wandering in the desert for 40 years. Moses sent Joshua and Caleb, along with represent-atives from each tribe, to inspect the land. Joshua and Caleb came back excited while the others complained and gave a poor report about the inhabitants of the land (13:26-33).

Focus: Joshua and Caleb responded that God will be with them and not to be concerned or afraid. However, the people were afraid and rebelled against God. Despite God's provisions out of Egypt, the parting of the Red Sea and 40 years in the wilderness. The Israelites continued not trusting and obeying God (14:20-22).

How to Apply: My wife and I had three personal confrontations with cancer. Like the Jews checking the promised land, we felt overwhelmed in the early stages. This tested our faith but through prayer and the support of others, we knew God was with us and would provide for us. We could not imagine dealing with cancer on our own. During this week, think of an impossible situation that you or a friend are going through now. Spend time in prayer for your friend. Then give them a call or drop a note in the snail mail (more personal than an e-mail).

Overview: The Israelites were camped at the Jordan and ready to enter the land that God had promised them. Moses was giving the people instructions as people prepared to occupy the land. The key instructions were:

- obedience - 4:5
- becoming a great nation – 4:7-8
- remember and be thankful – 4:9
- avoid idols – 4:16-19
- know God's mercy – 4:31
- only one God – 4:35, 39
- remember God's blessing – 4:37-38

Focus: Israel always had problems being obedient and remembering what God did for them. God reminded them of their past history of disobedience and told them to stay obedient. In Deuteronomy, the Ten Commandments are listed again and Moses challenged the people to listen, learn and obey God's instructions (5:1). Being thankful will help us know how God has worked and will continue to work in our lives. God is always with us and He will never abandon us (4: 31)

How to Apply: Recently, I have tried to be thankful in the midst of my struggles with Parkinsons. God does help us grow and depend on Him through hard times. During this week, remember how you have grown and have seen God work through prior struggles.

Overview: While the Jews were in the wilderness, Moses went up to Mt. Sinai to receive the Ten Commandments from God. As you read the first few, you find that God was a jealous God and did not want to share the Jew's affection with any other gods or idols. The first four commandments, including the misuse of His name, cover our relationship with God. This includes honoring a day of rest. Commandments five through ten cover our relationships with others.

Focus: Three of them have a few more comments beyond the initial phrase. These include having no gods or idols in our way of knowing God (5:8), remembering to keep the Sabbath (5:12), and to not covet anything of our neighbor's or friend's property (5:21).

How to Apply: For myself, the one that jumps out is not to place any idol before God because of His love for me. This includes my abilities which are his and not mine. God's relationship with me should cover all my life. During this week, pick one to focus on and change or adjust an area of your life:

- Vs. 7-8   no idols or distraction.
- Vs. 11   a day of rest.
- Vs. 16-19   work on a relationship.
- Vs. 19-20   love your neighbor.

Overview: After Moses death (Deuteronomy (34:5-12), Joshua took over the leadership of the Israelites as they prepared to enter the Promised Land. Joshua gave them God's instructions advising them He will always be with them and be strong and courageous. Through Joshua, God assured them also of His presence. What does strong and courageous look like? Maybe like Jason's phrase in the movie Galaxy Quest: "never give up, never surrender". God is always in control.

Focus: God's Word is our tool for being strong and courageous. In verse 8, God gives us the following three challenges:

- study His word continually.
- meditate on His Word day and night.
- obey all that is written in it and your way will be successful.

The more we study His Word and learn about God, the closer our desires will match His desires in our lives. We work with Him for the fulfillment of His purpose for our lives.

How to Apply: During this week, pray and meditate through verses 8 and 9. Spend time in God's Word meditating on specific verses which help you grow in your relationship with God. Add these two verses to your verse reference list. I have about 90 verses listed on small cards that I have referenced over the years. Once in a while, my time with God may be to go over my verse list. Continue to grow your list of verses.

WEEK 16   Judges 2:1-23   Focus: 2:10

Overview: Israel started out obeying God and conquering the nations in the Promised Land. Then Joshua passed away and they began to disobey God. The next generation did not acknowledge God or remember the great things He had done for Israel (2:10-11). They did evil in the Lord's sight and began to lose battles with their enemies. They continued to worship idols and other gods. The Lord was angry and abandoned them, thus causing them loss of victory and land.

Focus: They began to be conquered by their enemies and placed into slavery. Israel became very stressed and discouraged. God sent Judges to rescue His people. They would turn back to God and if the judge died, they turned back to their sinful and corrupt ways. They were becoming blinded by their sins.

How to Apply: When the Israelites became blinded, they continued to sin. Sometimes pride gets in our way. We need to stay faithful to God and be obedient to Him. We must seek His way and not our way. Our trials through infertility required our need to trust God in the process, allowing Him to work in our lives. During this week, ask God to reveal to you an area of your life which needs to be refocused toward Him. Maybe there is an area where you continue to sin and need to return to Him. This may be a hobby, friends you hang around with, a distraction, certain magazines or a relationship. Pray that God would reveal that area and help you make a change in that area of your life.

Overview: The book of Ruth helps connect the genealogy of Christ. Naomi had a son named Obed, the father of Jesse, the father of David (4:17). Ruth was from Moab and became one of two daughters-in-law to Naomi. When Naomi lost her husband and two sons, she told her two daughters-in-law she was returning to her hometown of Bethlehem. Ruth said she would go with Naomi. This meant leaving her home and family.

Focus: Ruth had no intentions to go back to her hometown but insisted on staying with Naomi wherever she went (1:16-18). This commitment began a lifelong relationship. Ruth committed herself to Naomi in Jerusalem as a foreigner far away from her homeland. Ruth did not go back to her homeland and she remained faithful to Naomi.

How to Apply: Close relationships can help us through hard circumstances. Ruth and Naomi's relationship included love, wisdom and commitment. Do you have any close relationships? Do you have any long-term relationships you are working on? When we lived in Rochester, NY, I had a close friend. We met almost weekly to encourage, support one another and have fun together. My job eventually moved us to Chicago. Now when we talk, it is like old times. During this week, pray about ensuring you have at least one close relationship that you can depend on (if married other than your spouse). Ask God to reveal who you can approach to begin building that relationship.

Overview: With all God did for the Israelites, they continued to disobey Him and allowed other gods, greed and perverted justice to prevail (8:6-8). Samuel was much later in the list of judges that God had sent. The Israelites demanded a king similar to other nations. Samuel became frustrated with the disobedient people and their request for a king.

Focus: But God comforted Samuel since this was not because of him but the people had also rejected God himself. God told Samuel to warn them on how a king would treat them. The king would mistreat their families and farmland. Yet, Israel, continued to demand a king.

How to Apply: There are two lessons in this situation. First, they continued to disobey God. Second, they would not listen to God. Like the Israelites, our desires often blind us to God's direction. He talks or directs us, and we again will not listen. During this week, pray through a time when you asked God for something and He said no and yet you persisted. Ask Him to help you listen and obey Him, so He can lead you purposely to live for Him. As you grow to love and know Him, your desires will match His desires for your life. Thus, your prayers begin to be answered. He does demand our attention and our obedience. My life is not less hectic but peaceful when I follow His way and not my own. An ongoing process is to have my desires match what He wants for my life.

WEEK 19 1 Samuel 12:1-13:1 Focus: 12:14-15

Overview: God instructed Joshua to lead the Israelites into the Promised Land. When they forgot God, they sinned before him and were conquered by some of the nations in the land. Israel became influenced by the other nations who did not follow God but followed their own evil desires. They cried out to God and confessed their sins. Samuel was one of the judges who God had sent to help the Israelites. The people asked for a king. God said if they would obey and follow Him, they would defeat the local nations and all would go well.

Focus: If they did not obey Him, God would bring His hand heavy down on them. Samuel warned the people to love God and worship Him and not to turn their back on Him. They were God's chosen nation and He was faithful, merciful and did not abandon them despite their disobedience. God was clear: continue to sin and you will be destroyed.

How to apply: Today our challenge is to continue to listen and obey. Sometimes when I need to seek His forgiveness for some anger issues, I delay doing this. This sends me down my path and not His. I must confess my struggle, trust in Him to show me the way out and return to following Him. During this week, pray about an area in your life where you continue to be tempted to sin. Ask God to reveal the sin and the way out (1 Corinthians 10:13).

Overview: Now God became very displeased with Saul, Israel's first king. God rejected Saul as their king. God then advised Samuel to go to Bethlehem and seek out Jesse who had eight sons. God would have Samuel anoint one of his sons as king of Israel. Jesse brought all of his sons, one at a time, before Samuel. God told Samuel no to the first seven sons. Samuel asked if these were all his sons. Jesse said he had one more son, and he brought his one younger son in from the fields.

Focus: God told Samuel to anoint this youngest and smallest son, David, as the new king. God does not look or judge people on their outward physical appearance. God looks into a person's heart to evaluate with his thoughts and intentions (16:7).

How to Apply: Is your heart toward God? What are your priorities? When I first started to run, my heart was focused more on the discipline of running and to get and stay in shape. I would get my workout in even if I missed my Bible reading. My priorities were my physical health and my relationship with God took a back seat. I needed to evaluate priorities and if God was first in every area of my life. During this week, use verse 16:7 as a meditation verse and add to your verse reference list. Consider your priorities and where God is in your life. Who abides in and controls your heart?

Overview: Solomon, David's son was now the third king of Israel. David wanted to build God's temple in Jerusalem for Israel's burnt offerings. He begins the preparation by gathering blocks of stone, iron for the nails, bronze for the doors and other building materials. However, God told David that Solomon would build God's temple (22:9). Solomon was to follow His instructions, and God would grant him success.

Focus: God emphasized Solomon's obedience to God. If Solomon obeys the laws, he would be successful. Through God, David advised Solomon to seek the Lord with all his heart. With God's guidance and a specific plan, Solomon did complete the project during his reign.

How to Apply: God challenges Solomon to be strong and courageous (22:13). In any large undertaking, seeking God will help you through it. The details of our two relocations seemed so overwhelming. But like the building of the temple, God was with us in every phase of our moves. God's hand was present as we loaded the truck in the middle of an ice storm to travel from Wilmington, Delaware to Rochester, New York. During this week, reread 22:13 and ask God for strength and courage as you face a current situation in your life. This could include a career change, leaving home for the first time, first year as empty nesters, your child leaving for college, retirement and ongoing health issues. This list could be endless.

WEEK 22   1 Kings 3:1-28 Focus: 1 Kings 3:9

Overview: With some Old Testament background, Solomon was still king of Israel. Saul, David and Solomon each reigned as king for forty years. Solomon loved the Lord and followed God's instructions. While building the temple, they still used other altars for sacrifices. The most important one was at Gibeon. Solomon went and offered 1,000 burnt offerings to God. One night, Solomon had a dream. Because of his obedience, God asked Solomon what he wanted and God would grant his request. Solomon considered God's request.

Focus: Solomon replied he needed help in governing the large nation of Israel. He asked for a wise and understanding mind to know the difference between right and wrong. God granted Solomon this request. God was so pleased with his request, God granted Solomon a long life of riches and honor. No other king in the world would be greater than Solomon. Check out the story of Solomon's wisdom with the two moms in 3:16-28.

How to Apply: What would you ask for from God? Riches? New house or car? Wisdom for the next season of your life? Our prayers usually ask for good health, help with a decision, bigger house, bigger car and a plethora of other requests. My wife and I include this phrase in our prayers: "Lord, continue to use us in the lives of others". Now that I am retired, our prayers include asking for direction in this season of our lives. During this week, consider what you would ask God for specifically and ask for it!

Overview: The book of Psalms has been called the written hymnal of the Bible. God knows us in detail and can give us hope in our darkest seasons. David wrote most of them. Many of the Psalms can be used for prayer and meditation, as well as for hymns. In Psalm 1, David challenges us to follow Him and not the path of the sinners who have no place with the godly. The believers are heading to life and the wicked are headed toward condemnation.

Focus: David gives us a visual of a tree planted near a river, where it bears fruit every year. This tree continues to prosper due to the access to the "living" water (1:3). David tells us of the wicked being scattered like worthless chaff and heading to destruction. They will be condemned at the time of judgment (1:4-6).

How to Apply: The wicked do not fare well with God. At times, I feel like I am off His path due to some distractions and too busy to spend time in His Word or too busy to pray. As I picture the tree getting nourishment from the water, I imagine that I must remain close to God and reconnect to His "living" water. I will find His comfort and strength. During this week, review verse 1:6 and see if you are on God's path for you or have you slid off the path? What do you need to do to reconnect to God and get back on His path?

WEEK 24 Psalm 119:161-176 Focus: 119:164

Overview: : Most of the Psalms were written by David and one was actually written by Moses (Psalm 90). Psalm 119 is the longest chapter in the Bible and expresses adoration for God and His Word. The writer's advice on God's Word includes knowing His Word (119:11), meditation (119:48), guidance (119:105) and a longing (119:131). This is a great Psalm to read the whole chapter out loud in prayer to God.

Focus: Verses 161 to 176 somewhat summarize the Psalm. This includes praise of God, request for discernment and delight in His Word. I find the acronym "ACTS" helpful as a guide when I pray:

> A (adoration)
>
> C (confession)
>
> T (thanksgiving)
>
> S (supplication).

How to Apply: During this week:

1) Spend some time praising and worshipping God using His Word and even a CD with some worship songs.
2) Spend some time with ACTS, and do not ask for any requests.
3) Spend time praying for others and not yourself.

Overview: Solomon wrote most of the book of Proverbs when he was still following and obeying God. Toward the end of his reign as king, Solomon became distracted with idolatry and materialism. This collection of wise sayings, point to seeking wisdom and discernment when making decisions in our lives. Our focus needs to be on knowing His Word, seeking His wisdom and guidance, allowing Him to guide us (2:9-11).

Focus: Proverbs also includes instructions on conduct and good vs. evil, the rich vs. the poor, etc. Seeking God's wisdom is a daily challenge for all choices and decisions we make. In 4:20 to 5:1, God wants us to "pay attention" to what He says (4:20, 5:1). He wants us to know His Word in our hearts, seek His wisdom, seek His path, watch our language and not be distracted.

How to Apply: I have used these eight verses as a prayer for a few weeks now. During this week, pray these verses to begin your day with him:

- 4:20-22   "pay attention" to Him.
- 4:23   know Him in your heart
- 4:24   watch your language.
- 4:25-27   avoid distractions.
- 5:1   seek His wisdom.

:

WEEK 26 Ecclesiastes 11:1-10   Focus: 11:4

Overview: Solomon is believed to be the author of this book, and it was written toward the end of his life when he was apart from God and involved with idolatry and materialism. Chapter 11 tells us to do anything we want but remember that we must give an account to God for all we do (11:9). We must maintain our relationship and walk with God.

Focus: Be intentional about doing something God has directed you to do without hesitation (11:4). Try to serve in a variety of ways because you may never know what will work (verses 11:6). You may never see and miss the outcome if you hesitate.

How to Apply: My favorite word is intentional. We must be willing to do what we say we will do and also do want God wants. Many ideas lose their focus once we decide to wait for the perfect conditions (11:4). Each season of my life brings new challenges, choices and opportunities. I must choose to act in His will and purpose to continue to move forward. At the age of 65, I still have a good 20 years left – God willing! During this week, reread verse 4. Consider where you feel God is leading you. Is your faith nudging you to step out in trust or to move out of your comfort zone? Take action now and stop talking and praying about it. Remember, God will want us to be accountable for all we do or don't do.

Overview: Most scholars believe Solomon wrote this book early in his reign. This is the story of God as the source of love paralleled to the loving and romantic relationship between a man and women. Through God, we would define this love as real and genuine. Think of the challenging relationship in a marriage as you read the heart felt and emotional dialogue. The passion, desire and true love for one another is powerful throughout the book. This is in contrast to the worldly self-love and exploited sexual relationships which are beyond any areas of commitment.

Focus: The young man admonishes her with comments including her eyes are like doves, her hair falling like waves, her perfect teeth and lips like a ribbon of scarlet (4:1-3). The young woman admonishes him with comments including his head is like gold, his hair is wavy, his eyes like jewels and lips like perfumed lilies (5:10-13). God wants to be the center of our marriage and our love for Him and each other. As I read the whole book, I felt God's love encourage me to show my wife, Patti, the same God's love.

How to Apply: This book reminds not to take my wife for granted - even after 40 years. During this week, as a stretch read all eight chapters of this book. If you are married, think of your spouse as you read the book. If you are single, read it to God. Be focused on genuine love. Meditate on God's love rather than the love defined by this world.

Overview: This book is about Job who went through some severe struggles. Job was a righteous man and God allowed Satan to take his wealth, his children, his reputation and his health from Job. Satan was certain Job would then turn his back on God (2:5-7). Throughout the book, Job has conversations with God and questions God. We read conversations with God and his three friends who only criticize him and were no support or encouragement to Job.

Focus: Job does begin to turn back to God, stating the fear of the Lord is true wisdom and we know true evil to avoid (28:28). Whatever our circumstances, God is with us. Job questions God and does not always get an answer about God's plan. At the end of the book, Job returns to God. God blesses Job with even more than he had before his countless trials. (42:10).

How to Apply: In verses 38:1-3, God asks Job who he is to question His wisdom. He talks to Job with a series of questions regarding who He is, what He has done and who knows the "law of the universe and how God rules the earth" (38:33). I have used this chapter for worship and thanking God for His past, present and future blessings in my life. God is sovereign and even in life's worst trials. He has always been with me. Spend time reading through this chapter. You can use the verses for prayers, meditation and worship. The verses are written as questions, as God confronted Job for questioning His wisdom.

Overview: Here is more Old Testament background. When Jacob, father of Joseph, came to Egypt, he came with all his sons. These sons became the 12 tribes of Israel who Moses would eventually lead from Egypt. During the reign of Solomon, two of the tribes did not follow Solomon. Judah and Benjamin separated from the other ten tribes. They called themselves Judah (southern kingdom) and the other ten remained as Israel (northern kingdom). This was the beginning of the collapse of both kingdoms.

Focus: In this chapter, God was not pleased with Israel. Israel continued to sin against God, to worship other gods and be influenced and following the ways of the nearby pagan nations. After Solomon, the next twenty kings were all bad and did not follow God. Consequences of their disobedience, resulted in Assyria bringing the Israelites into captivity. Israel received the full punishment from God for their continued disobedience.

How to Apply: Have you ever felt abandoned by God? When cancer impacted our marriage three times, we longed for His presence and reassurance. Our fears initially overwhelmed and blinded us. When we put our trust in God, we overcame our fears. He brought us comfort and peace. Pray using verses 13 and 14. Do not reject Him in your blindness. Ask God to provide you with direction and trust in Him as you continue to obey and grow in Him.

Overview: Judah was in the same situation as Israel. They were not following God despite all God had done for them. God had saved them from Egypt, watched over them, brought them into the Promised Land and gave them military victories over the surrounding nations. They also refused to listen. Judah had twenty kings, with only six good and fourteen bad. The kings continued to fail the people as God had told them would happen. God told them kings would not be good for them.

Focus: God sent the Babylonians to conquer Jerusalem and to destroy God's temple. Now both Israel and Judah were in captivity. Both tribes were reprimanded by the prophets Isaiah, Jeremiah and Ezekiel. The prophet's relationships with God allowed them to be grounded in God not influenced by others around them.

How to Apply: God's anger and justice had placed Israel and Judah in exile due to their ongoing disobedience (24:20). Are you spending time in His Word to be grounded in His obedience? God's people lost focus and had lost touch with Him. After two surgeries for Parkinsons, I was diagnosed with Prostate Cancer. My first reaction was "God please leave me alone for a few months." I sought His strength and focused on His mercies which helped me through 45 radiation treatments. Final result was cancer free! Verse 24:20 reminds us of His anger and justice as a result of disobedience.

WEEK 31   Joel 2:12-32   Focus: 2:12

Overview: Joel prophesized during a time of peace and
prosperity. However, Judah still was not following God. Joel
has two key messages. First, God would continue His invitation
to repentance and second, in the day of the Lord, all will
acknowledge God or face judgment. Those who decide to
reject God will face this judgment in the final days. The Lord
desires His people to repent and offers salvation when we call
on Him (2:32).

Focus: He will save and restore Judah and take pity in His
people (2:18-19). He is a God of mercy and is gracious, slow to
anger and full of kindness (2:13). God wants relationships with
us and not rituals. God wants our hearts to turn to him and not
just go through the motions with physical evidence as torn
clothes or offerings.

How to Apply: Recently, our pastor added about one minute of
quiet meditation into our morning services. This time of
reflection has been very precious to me since it is sometimes
hard to slow down during the week. This challenged me to do
this at home also. We must add some quiet moments of
reflection with God into our schedule a few times during the
week. We must intentionally take time to be quiet and listen to
Him. During this week, spend time with God, share your day
with Him and praise Him. Meditate or think through Joel 2:12
and Psalm 46:10.

WEEK 32   Jonah 2:1-10   Focus: 2:7

Overview: Jonah was told by God to go to Nineveh which was the most important city in Assyria. God told Jonah to tell the people of Nineveh of God's judgment because He saw their wickedness. Jonah was afraid they would repent if he talked to them. Jonah went in the opposite direction and through a series of circumstances, found himself in the belly of a big fish. He was feeling disillusioned and hopeless. Jonah called out to God and thought he was near death and would never be in God's presence again (2:4-5). God does hear his cry and responds (2:6-7).

Focus: One time I worked 12-hour night shifts for about 32 of 33 days. We did get 8 hours off on Christmas! I also had a two-hour commute. I prayed to God to rescue me even though the shifts did not end right away. He did respond and give me endurance and confidence that change would come in His time. Prayer changed me and not the circumstance.

How to Apply: Have you ever felt hopeless and cried out to God? God does hear our prayers (2:7). He may not answer our way but will help our faith grow. During this week, meditate on 2:7, remembering God will respond, just as He responded to Jonah (2:10). Press forward knowing that God will hear you and respond to you as sure as the rains will come in the spring and the morning sun will rise (Hosea 6:3).

Overview: Amos was a prophet, shepherd and fig grower. He was around Israel the time when they were not following the Lord. Being exiled into Assyria was not too far away. The first one and a half chapters of Amos tell of God's judgment on the surrounding nations, who have sinned again and again. In the middle of chapter two, God again also tells Israel and Judah they are disobedient, not listening and "have sinned again and again" (2:4, 6).

Focus: In chapter four, God tells the people all the disasters He will bring down on them because of their continued disobedience. God sent all kinds of disasters, "but still" (repeated five times in this chapter) they refused to listen to God. God then tells Amos to stop preaching to them. For their refusal to listen, the people would be sent into captivity (7:17).

How to Apply: Sometimes listening can be hard for me because I focus on my response to others and am not really listening. I want to fix whatever my wife, daughters or friends are sharing. They may only need a listening ear. This is the same with God. It is too easy to come to Him just for our requests. We must treat God for who He is and with reverence. During this week, meditate on who He is and worship Him without asking for anything personal. This is a challenge to spend five minutes in silence to allow Him to speak. Use 4:13 as a reference during your time with God. His name is the Lord God Almighty.

Overview: Hosea is written during the final awful days when Israel is close to going into exile. He compares God as the husband and Israel as the no longer loving or faithful wife. God will block her way and she will not be able to find her lovers (2:6-7). He will show His unfailing love and compassion. Despite Israel's refusal to obey God, He remains faithful to His chosen people.

Focus: Even as they are close to exile, God gives Israel hope and wants to forgive them, build a relationship with them and be faithful to them. A broken relationship is painful – whatever the origin. God will grow Israel, be their God and Israel will be God's people (2:23). Since God brought Israel out of Egypt and guided them, they remained disobedient and worshipped other gods. God still loved Israel despite their sinfulness.

How to Apply: Sometimes it is easy to drift from God when our busy schedules leave no time for Him. When things are going well, I could be drifting away from Him almost without knowing. I am too busy to spend time in His word and soon I had not read His Word for two or three days. My purpose for daily time in His Word is to be grounded for every season. During this coming week, rate yourself as following, drifting or not following your relationship with God. Goal is a more steady follower. Evaluate the quality of your time with Him and see who is the pilot of your every day life. Reference verses 19-20.

WEEK 35   Micah 7:1-20   Focus: 7:18-20

Overview: Micah gives us an update on God putting Israel and Judah on trial for their continued sins. Micah predicts the downfall of the Jews along with the destruction of Samaria and Jerusalem (1:3-5). Micah gives them hope in their future. Micah predicts the coming of Jesus from the town of Bethlehem.

Focus: Micah tells the people God is not looking for more offerings or one's firstborn. God wants what is right and just, showing mercy and walking humbly with Him (6:8). God seeks a close relationship with His children.

How to Apply: I do not want to get caught going through the motions or lacking sincerity in my relationship. Humility and surrendering is a work in progress. My relationship should permeate every area of my life including church attendance and serving at church as well as at home. During this week, spend some quality time with God asking Him to impact every area of your life including the following:

- Family.
- Technology – from Facebook to tv to movies?
- Time use – prioritize to be effective.
- Kid's sports – practice on Sunday?
- Friends – what influence do they have?
- Pick one, pray and adjust as needed.

Overview: Nahum wrote to the people of Judah and predicted the judgment on Nineveh, the capital of Syria. This city was repeatedly warned of their sinfulness. The Lord is a jealous God and slow to anger. Yet His power is great and never lets the guilty have free reign (1:2-3). God's Word applies to individuals as well as to nations. God rules over the world and all of the nations and also wants a close relationship with all individuals.

Focus: The United States is in a downward moral spiral. Protests are motivated by hatred, violence, prejudice, shootings and anti-God. God and His name has been removed from schools, governments and businesses – our history. Nahum brings hope for Judah in the past and for the United States today. God comes when there is trouble and knows who trust Him. He also brings an overwhelming flood over His enemies. Our country needs to seek and find refuge in Him.

How to Apply: During this week, pray for this country and its leaders. Start with the President (no matter who he is!) and for the Supreme Court, Congress, local politicians, principals, school officials, teachers and families. Pray for those serving in the military, the veterans and for someone you may know currently serving. Pray for them during your prayer time. Make a list by name for reference. As a stretch, read all of the three chapters of Nahum and see what happens to Nineveh.

Overview: Habakkuk sees a world of violence, sin and no mercy. He calls to God for help. There is no justice where the wicked outnumber the righteous (1:1-4). He attempts to understand God's plan. Will the righteous continue to suffer and the wicked go unpunished forever? How can God work good through any of this? God does not give us all the answers right away. Sometimes His answers are yes, no or wait.

Focus: God tells Habakkuk to wait and endure. Waiting for His timing is one of the hardest subjects in the Bible. God's timing is rarely in sync with our timetable and Habakkuk was no exception. God's timing is always perfect and how often do we see that is true. In chapter three, Habakkuk prays to God and realizes how awesome He is and how God will come when his people are in deep need. God is our strength, and He will make us surefooted as the deer. He keeps us on His path.

How to Apply: On my morning run, I occasionally see deer along the wooded path. They have amazing agility and my sudden appearance has never caused one to stumble. Are you as surefooted as a deer? Confirm with God that you are sure-footed on His path and not stumbling with your plans. Stay firm and grounded in His Word to endure waiting on His timing. Ask God to reveal how you can spend more time consistently in His Word. Review 3:18-19.

WEEK 38   Zephaniah 2:1-15   Focus: 2:1-3

Overview: Zephaniah tells Judah to repent. He prophesized during the reign of King Josiah, tried to turn him and the nation of Judah back to God. The Lord's wrath, anger and power were going to bring judgment on Judah and Jerusalem. He will sweep away the people and animals and reduce humanity to rubble (2:1-4). In Chapter 2, God brings His judgment on many nations. Zephaniah challenges God's people to repent before the fury and anger of the Lord begins on the day of destruction.

Focus: Zephaniah warns the people that God may yet save them from their own sinful ways which may lead to their destruction. Throughout the Old Testament, we see a pattern not much different from today: sinning, in trouble, call for help which leads to repenting. Personally, I need to start every day with Him without exception. I believe starting ten minutes a day with God is better than one hour once per week with Him.

How to Apply: Zephaniah's instructions (2:3) are similar to Micah's instructions in Micah 6:8, accept for the addition that Zephaniah tells us to act now (2:2). God's directions to us are to seek justice, seek mercy and to walk humbly with Him. Pray for His guidance as you evaluate your time usage. Set aside and even schedule some daily time to commune with God in His Word.

Overview: The nation of Edom always had contempt for Israel. As Israel was traveling from Egypt to the Promised Land, the Edomites denied them permission to take a shorter route through Edom. Now the Babylonians were attacking Jerusalem and Edom was happy to see them defeated and sent into exile under Babylonian rule. Pride was strong in Edom as they gloated over Jerusalem's and Israel's demise.

Focus: God sent Obadiah to warn Edom that God's wrath and their judgment and downfall are coming, and God will destroy Edom because of their pride. Pride can sneak into your life quietly as you are slowly changing your thinking. God does not see pride as a virtue, and He will bring you down when you consider yourself better than others (Philippians 2:3-4).

How to Apply: This applies to individuals as well as nations. The 2018 Winter Olympic games were almost done and the athletes were full of pride and excited representing their nations. Some of their pride overshadowed their performance resulting in unfavorable publicity for the countries they represented. During this week, ask God to reveal any area of your life where your thoughts do not line up with Philippians 2:3-4. Add this area to your prayer list to pray for your needed adjustment.

WEEK 40   Isaiah 26:1-21 Focus: 26: 12,13

Overview: The prophet Isaiah's time was when the Assyrians were becoming a major threat to Israel. This book is mountain and valley time for Israel. In their valley, Judah continued to disobey, reject and ignore God (1:2-4). The city of Jerusalem was also unfaithful and were murderers. They refused to help orphans and widows (1:21-23). Isaiah tells of the mountain top relationship with God, when God will welcome them back, forgiven, with harsh judgments upon their enemies.

Focus: In chapter 26, Israel praises God for their deliverance. He is a God of peace, justice, trust and righteousness (26;12-13). Isaiah gives us four tips for our spiritual lives:

- Vs.3, 12   He will give us peace.
- Vs. 12   All we have is from God.
- Vs. 13   Others are our leaders.
- Vs. 13   We worship God alone.

How to Apply: I try to give thanks for all He has given me and to seek His peace and to worship Him even when I do not understand. I have felt frustrated when things do not go my way. Yet, He gives me greater peace when I honor Him first and allow Him to work His purpose in my life. During this week, praise and honor God before asking for something.

Overview: Isaiah portrays a harsh God of judgment and justice who will destroy the enemies of Israel and Judah. He is also a God of mercy and forgiveness and will forget their sins and restore His people (43:25). They are His chosen people. Chapter 43 tells of God as their Savior, their help and will bring them victory. Isaiah reinforces God's protection by recounting their history. He is the Lord and will destroy the Babylonians just as He destroyed the army of Egypt below the waves (43:16-17).

Focus: He can help us today through trials and struggles. He has personally helped us particularly through cancer and recently, Parkinsons. We were praying as we watch for God's direction and timing. He has guided us through situations in the past, and we believe and trust He will be there again for us.

How to Apply: During this week, whatever situation you are currently in, remember to trust Him even when you do not understand. He will not let you go even when you feel like you are under the waves or being consumed by the fire. Let God's peace and presence surround you as you seek His trust and protection through Him (43:2). Pray through verse two being reminded God will change you first and will assist you through the waters. God can give us more than we can handle, so we put our faith in Him and not ourselves.

Overview: Jeremiah spoke to Judah and the southern kingdom during the reigns of the last five kings. As time approached for the Babylonians to take them into exile, Jeremiah spoke two overall messages in his book. First, Judah continues to be disobedient, does not listen to God and totally rejects Him (9:2). God hints to vanquish Judah into exile and make Jerusalem and their other towns like ghost towns for not following Him.

Focus: Second, Jeremiah does talk of hope for the people including forgiveness, justice and God's unfailing love for them. God desires for Judah to boast in knowing Him first. He is a just and righteous God and delights in loving His people by showing His unfailing love. Knowing God starts in three specific areas as challenged and encouraged through this book.

How to Apply: The three areas are:

1) Read the Bible daily.
2) Meditate with your list of reference verses.
3) Pray daily with your request list.

Pick number one to work on by starting or scheduling daily time to read His Word. Many Bibles suggest reading programs to help you get started.

WEEK 43   Jeremiah 17:1-27   Focus: 17:8

Overview: Jeremiah continues to write of the peoples' sin and their rejection of God. God's anger for their continued disobedience leads Him to send them as captives into exile (17:4). Jeremiah remained a faithful prophet, despite the people not heeding His warnings. (17:14-15). They did not observe the Sabbath and His judgment would come if they did not respond to obey God and observe the Sabbath.

Focus: God continues to speak of the hope and confidence to bless those whose complete trust is in Him. God uses the example of a tree planted near a river - grounded and growing from the river's water. The roots go down deep and the tree continues to survive the heat and months of drought as it grows and produces fruit annually. Reminds me of my website: Grounded and Growing.

How to Apply: Prayer is an important part of growing our relationship with God. Referencing the three areas from last week, work on areas two and three. My wife and I are working on our prayer life. First, we stopped reading books on prayer and started to pray together. Second, we set my cell phone alarm for 7:00 PM every night as a reminder to pray. Now we usually pray before the alarm goes off. Seek God's leading as you think on 17:8. Prayer is communicating with God.

WEEK 44   Lamentations 3:1-66   Focus: 3:22-26

Overview: Jeremiah writes to Judah and the southern kingdom and tells of the destruction of Jerusalem. We see some key discouraging words throughout this book. His words include: sinned, affliction, anger, dark, helpless, suffering, grief and rebellion. Jeremiah was lamenting over the punishment and condition of the people of Jerusalem. In an extended reading for this week of chapter three, these words are replaced with uplifting hope as he continues.

Focus: Some of Jeremiah's encouraging words include: love, hope, compassion, faithfulness, mercies, repentance, salvation and waiting. These words give us hope and lift our spirits. One of the words is "waiting" (3:25-26). Waiting for God to work in His timing can be difficult in some circumstances. In the midst of my kidney stones, I was miserable and I could not find a comfortable position to sleep. Finally, after six days, I passed the stones and had immediate relief. Thank you, Lord!

How to Apply: During this week, read Chapter three aloud to help you listen better and read slower. Review the list of key words and see what words jump out at you or impact your thoughts. Waiting is a common word for myself. God continues to teach me to emphasize waiting for His timing in my life and not my wishes or personal comfort.

WEEK 45 Ezekiel 11:1-25   Focus: 11:18-19

Overview: Ezekiel's message is a reality check for the Jews. They expected God to save His people and the city of Jerusalem. Their expectations of God were very different from His plans for them. They continued to sin and promote injustice so God placed them in exile in Babylon. Ezekiel's message is continued disobedience has consequences, and God told Ezekiel to tell the Jews that they would be judged and scattered. God's plan continues to move forward.

Focus: Yet God does tell them because of His mercy they will be gathered back together. When they return home, they will remove their idols. God will give them a singleness of heart and a new spirit (11:18-19). This would be a slow process because they were still listening to evil leaders (11:2-3) and believed they did not need God (14:2-3). Despite their stubbornness, God's love prevails (20:16-17).

How to Apply: Are you continuing to have distractions from idols or other activities keeping you from obeying God? He wants to help us remove our idols. Facebook is a very good tool for keeping in touch with others and sharing pictures. Facebook had the potential of becoming a habit, and I am now limiting my time and working on some boundaries. Check areas of your life for distractions and allow God to give you a singleness of heart for Him (11:19).

WEEK 46   Daniel 2:1-49   Focus: 2:20-23

Overview: The book of Daniel gives some prophecies of the end times and hope for the Jews who were exiled in Babylon. Daniel also tells of his sincere walk with God and realizing God's daily presence in his life. Chapter one tells about possible advantages of being a vegetarian. Additional Daniel adventures include dream interpretation (2:45) and lion's den survivor (6:19-22). Daniel survived circumstances through his daily trust and walk with God.

Focus: How does Daniel's faith and trust match up against our walk with God? Do we limit God or make Him a small God? Seven verses in Daniel show his daily walk and relationship with God as he sought His presence in his life every day.

How to Apply: Review these references to see how God can work in your life:

- Vs. 1:9   Chief official favored him
- Vs. 2:18   Asked God for mercy.
- Vs. 2:28   There is a God in heaven.
- Vs. 2:30   Know God is working.
- Vs. 2:45   Working through Daniel.
- Vs. 3:17   God will rescue them.
- Vs. 2:20-23   God is sovereign.

Referencing 2:20-23, spend time thinking on these verses of who God is through praise. My prayer for us is we will not limit God or limit what He can do working through us.

Overview: Persia is now in control over the Babylonians. The king of Persia felt sorry for the Jews. He allowed them to return to Jerusalem and the they continued not to obey God. They lived in nice houses and planted but harvested very little (1:3-6). God's temple remains in shambles. God wanted to return as the top priority in their lives, specifically with rebuilding of His temple and the city walls.

Focus: How are things with you? Is God a priority in every area of your life? Are you sitting back and waiting? Sometimes God wants us to wait as He did for the Jews in exile before He rescued them. Other times He calls us to action. The Jews needed to set priorities. As a work in progress, I try to check my priorities to ensure they match God's path for my life. I intentionally watch my daily choices including books I read, movies I watch, people I associate with and how I use my time.

How to Apply: One item Patti and I agree on is to be careful what we put into our minds. With the exception of the movie "The Passion", directed by Mel Gibson, we do not watch or attend R rated movies. I have heard you can look at your checkbook, the books and movies on your shelf and your calendar schedule. This will give you an idea of how important God is in your life. During this week, consider how much God is a priority in your life. See what areas need changing or adjusting.

WEEK 48   Zechariah 1:1-17   Focus: 1:17

Overview: Zechariah, like Haggai, writes to the Jewish exiles returning to Jerusalem to rebuild God's temple. His first eight chapters cover God's encouragement and blessings to the returnees. The last six chapters cover God's big picture plan and mentions the coming Messiah and the future of Jerusalem (12:9-10, 14:10-11). God's plan for Israel is restoration through repentance as Zerubbabel will lead the rebuilding (4:6-8).

Focus: God will show mercy on Israel and Jerusalem and will rebuild His temple and bring prosperity to Israel (1:16-17). During this time, God showed more of His mercy and forgiveness through the leadership of Haggai, Zechariah, Ezra and Nehemiah. Does an area of your life need rebuilding?

How to Apply: During my challenge with Parkinson's, God did help me work through His plan, gave me hope and a peace that only He can give. He showed me His mercy and to trust Him with my health. After one surgery of 4 ½ hours while awake, a second surgery of 2 hours asleep and some power pack programming, I am now 98% free of any shaking or tremors. Ask God to reveal what area of your life may need adjusting or rebuilding (1:17) and begin praying and working on it this week.

WEEK 49   Esther 4:1-17   Focus: 4:14

Overview: The book of Esther was written during the time when the descendants of those that were in exile were then under Persian rule (1:1-2). God is not mentioned in this book but is clearly working behind the scenes. A man named Haman was plotting against the Jews (3:1-2). Esther was the queen as appointed by the king. Uncle Mordecai contacted Esther and she learned of the plot against Esther and Mordecai's people. (4:7-8).

Focus: Esther's faith overcame her fears. She risked her life to go before the king. Mordecai mentioned that Esther may have been appointed queen "for just such a time as this" (4:14). God's guidance and protection leads His children through all circumstances and can do this behind the scenes.

How to Apply: When we first decided to join our current church, God was working behind the scenes. This church had an interim pastor and was searching for a permanent one. With both moves, we chose between two churches and picked the one different from the previous church. God called Esther" For such a time as this". God uses the least likely people to do His greatest work. Reread the passage. Is God calling you to step forward in faith in your life? Are you prepared to say yes to His calling? You may be needed for such a time as this (4:14).

Overview: Ezra continues the story of the exiles to Jerusalem with three parts. The first part was through Zerubbabel, as reported through Zechariah, the second part was through Ezra and the third part was through Nehemiah. Israel received support from the king of Persia who issued a decree for their return. The hand of God was with Ezra when he returned to Jerusalem to continue to rebuild the temple and to teach God's Word to the people (7:8-10).

Focus: The king of Persia gave Ezra everything he asked for and needed, along with governing authority through the king's decree. God shows we can count on His promises. With their spiritual life, Israel was given a chance for a fresh start from their past. God again intervened in Israel's history. However, some of the people were still intermarrying with other nations and were distracted and not following God (9:1-2).

How to Apply: God's promises are true and we can count on them. Through my many (and more) seasons of life, God continues to help me grow. Moving into retirement, I do not want to get stuck in a pattern but seek to ensure I am doing what He wants me to do. He shows me He can do the impossible, and I must trust in Him to work beyond my thoughts and plans. Can you think of a time when you faced an impossible situation and God led you through it? He is the God of the impossible and can use each of us.

Overview: God works through Nehemiah as he prays about returning to Jerusalem. He knows this will be a monumental task to rebuild the city walls. Nehemiah is portrayed as a man of prayer, a leader, an organizer, a communicator, planner, encourager and intentional with all his actions. Everyone gets involved from the king issuing the decree to the individuals and families working on the wall.

Focus: In chapter four, the enemies of the Jews are showing opposition to the rebuilding of the wall. This discourages the Jews at the wall. Nehemiah advises them that God will be with them and will fight for them. First, he reminds the people to remember and pray to God in four verses in chapter four (4:4,9,14,20). Second, Nehemiah adjusts his plan as circumstances change. He placed guards at the wall for protection for the workers (4:16).

How to Apply: Nehemiah is my second favorite book of the Bible (second to Philippians). I appreciate how Nehemiah channels everything through prayer. I found out I had prostate cancer and decided on 45 radiation treatment. At the end of the first week, I felt this would take forever. Through my prayers and the prayers of others I completed all the treatments. My follow up appointment was a PSA of ZERO! Pray about a season you are in now for God to be with you and make adjustments as He guides you through.

Overview: The final voice of the Old Testament is a book written by Malachi. Four hundred years would pass before we hear from John the Baptist (3:1). Malachi's message includes the Jews are still not completely following God. Again, God offers repentance (3:6-7) and a promise of mercy (3:17-18). Malachi tells the future where God will return and bring judgement on all those who deny Him.

Focus: Are you ready for His return? Do you need to return to Him first? Our spiritual growth to deepen our relationship with Him is a steady progression with ongoing adjustments in our lives. Disobedience will result in consequences and judgment.

How to Apply: During this week, evaluate your time usage to stay on course as listed below:

- Time in His Word.
- Time with your family.
- Time and commitment to church.
- Time on your computer/ I-pad/ cell phone.
- Time working on relationships—family & friends.

I checked the APPs on my phone and reduced the number. The biggest time waster for me was the ESPN APP. It has been deleted. Pick one of the above for this week. Or delete an APP!

Biblical References

Week 1	Genesis 1: 2:4
Week 2	Genesis 2:2-25
Week 3	Genesis 3:1-24
Week 4	Genesis 6:1-22
Week 5	Genesis 12;1-20
Week 6	Genesis 22:1-24
Week 7	Genesis 37:1-36
Week 8	Genesis 45:1-46:4
Week 9	Exodus 2:1-3:10
Week 10	Exodus 20:1-17
Week 11	Leviticus 7:1-38
Week 12	Numbers 14:1-45
Week 13	Deuteronomy 4:1-40
Week 14	Deuteronomy 5:1-33
Week 15	Joshua 1:1-18
Week 16	Judges 2:1-23

Week 35	Micah 7:1-20
Week 36	Nahum 1:1-15
Week 37	Habakkuk 3:1-19
Week 38	Zephaniah 2:1-15
Week 39	Obadiah 1-21
Week 40	Isaiah 26;1-21
Week 41	Isaiah 43:1-28
Week 42	Jeremiah 9:1-26
Week 43	Jeremiah 17:1-27
Week 44	Lamentations 3:1-66
Week 45	Ezekiel 11:1-25
Week 46	Daniel 2:1-49
Week 47	Haggai 1:1-15
Week 48	Zechariah 1:1-17
Week 49	Esther 4:1-17
Week 50	Ezra 7:1-28
Week 51	Nehemiah 4:1-23
Week 52	Malachi 3:1-18

Watch for Dale's next book!

Check his Verse of the Week on Facebook.

Visit his website:

www.groundedandgrowingweekly.com

Brief Old Testament Overview

(numbers are years in B.C.)

1 Samuel   Saul – King (1050)

               Saul – first king

               1 Samuel 9:15-17

2 Samuel   David – king (1010)

               David – second king   2 Samuel 2:1-7

1 Kings   Solomon – king (970)

               Solomon – third king   1 Kings 2:1-12

Divided Kingdom

NORTH

I Kings 11:11-13, 26, 37-40

Jeroboam

10 Tribes

20 kings

20 bad

209 years

SOUTH

2 Chronicles 10:1-19

Rehoboam

2 Tribes (Judah, Benjamin)

20 kings

6 good/ 14 bad

345 years

<u>NORTH</u>

2 Kings 17:1-8 (722)

Fall of Israel (Samaria)

To Assyria

<u>SOUTH</u>

2 Kings 25:1-5 (586)

Fall of Judah (Jerusalem)

to Babylon

Babylon conquers Assyria (612)

Jeremiah 25:11-14

Persia conquers Babylon (539)

Persia – issues Edict of Cyrus

Jews return to Jerusalem

2 Chronicles 36:20-23

Sets up return, reformation, rebuild

Jerusalem and rebuild temple.

Jeremiah 29:11-14, 31:1-6,

Deuteronomy 30:1-10

Old Testament Prayers and Sermons

Moses before the Promised Land

Deuteronomy 6:1-25

Joshua's farewell challenge
Joshua 24:1-15

Results of intermarriage

Ezra 9:5-15

Desolation of Jerusalem
Daniel 9:1-19

Confession of Israelites
Nehemiah 9:1-38

Judgement of Jerusalem
Lamentations

Devotional on Word of God

Psalm 119

Old Testament: God's Plan

God has a plan for each of His people and He begins to work in their lives. Below are examples on their calling from God.

Abraham called: Genesis 12:1-4

Joseph in Egypt: Genesis 45:3-7

Moses called: Exodus 3:11, 4:1, 10, 13

Joshua takes over: Joshua 1:1-9

Samuel called: 1 Samuel 3:1-21

Isaiah called: Isaiah 6:8

Jeremiah called: Jeremiah 1:4-8

Ezekiel called: Ezekiel 1:28 – 2:9

Nehemiah: Nehemiah 1:1-4, 2:4-5

Jonah called: Jonah 1:1-3

Old Testament Encouragement

Through God's love for us, we have a present and future hope. God in the Old Testament goes from the law and instructions to a relationship with Jesus in the New Testament.

His Word:

> Joshua 1:6-9, 1 Kings 2:3,
>
> Psalm 119:9-16

Trust in Him:

> Proverbs 3:5-6, Isaiah 26:3,
>
> Jeremiah 17:7-8

His Strength:

> Isaiah 41:10, Psalm 28:7,
>
> Habakkuk 3:18-19

His Power:

> 1 Samuel 17:44-47, Psalm 18:30-36,
>
> Daniel 2:20-23

His Faithfulness:

> Deuteronomy 7:9, 1 Kings 8:56-61,
>
> Lamentations 3:22-23

His Love:

> Nehemiah 1:5, Psalm 32:10,
>
> Psalm 57:9-10, Joel 2:13

Our Refuge:

> 2 Samuel 22:2-3, 31, Psalm 5:11-12,
>
> Psalm 64:10, Proverbs 2:6-8

Hope in Him:

> Isaiah 40:31, Psalm 33:20-21
>
> Psalm71:14-16, Micah 7:7-8

Only a devotion away………

From being grounded and growing in your relationship with God.

READ IT! LEARN IT! SHARE IT!

'One Week at a Time"

"Journey through the Old Testament"

VISIT:
www.groundedandgrowingweekly.com

Also, check out my Tuesday "Verse of the Week" on Facebook.

SAMPLE of Week 1 from next untitled book:

Day 1:   TRUST   Proverbs 3:5

"Trust in the LORD with all your heart
and lean not on your own understanding;
in all your ways submit to him,
and he will make your paths straight".

God is asking for complete trust with all of our hearts. During struggles in my life, I have tried to truly trust in Him completely and try not to ask for specific answers or attempt to understand how He will work. The more I wait for His answers, the better the situation goes. He may not always rectify the situation but I know He is with me. Pray today for complete trust and allow God to guide and keep you on His path for you and not your path. Acknowledge Him in all you do today and keep these two verses in mind. Think through what is happening at work, with your family or a difficult relationship you are in. Trust and submit to God. He may not always rescue you or resolve the situation this day but His peace will be with you throughout the day. Wait in His timing and in His peace for His answer.

28595145R00046

Made in the USA
Lexington, KY
20 January 2019